Social Enterprise

What it is and why it matters

Revised 2nd Edition

Comments on the First Edition

Very clearly written and informative. I've now passed it on to my Finance Manager.

Steve Gamgee Chief Executive, The Wallich , Homeless Charity

I read your book last week and almost wept - for 5 years I have been looking for a simple, plain speaking and down to earth book for my students - I now have it in your book!

Mike Bull, Centre for Enterprise, Manchester Metropolitan University Business School

Social Enterprise

What it is and why it matters

Revised 2nd Edition

by

Martin Price

FFLAN Ltd

First Edition First Published in Great Britain January 2008

Second Edition First Published in Great Britain November 2009

Copyright © Martin Price 2008, 2009

Published by:

Fflan Ltd
37 Cardiff Road, Dinas Powys, Vale of Glamorgan, Wales
CF64 4DH

The moral right of this author has been asserted

ISBN 978-1-905979-01-1

Printed in Great Britain by the MPG Books Group, Bodmin and King's Lynn

To my long-suffering family for whom this book has been a long time coming.

David
Angharad
Ieuan
Rhiannon
Eleri

and especially Nicky

Contents

		Page
Why this Book?		ix
Why a Second Edition?		
1.	What is Social Enterprise?	1
	a. A Quiz – What are these entities? Are they Social Enterprises?	
	b. Social Enterprise is not new	
	c. Values	
	d. Using the right words	
	• Social Firms	
	• Community Enterprise	
	• Development Trusts	
	• Cooperative	
2.	Not Social Enterprise	25
	a. Philanthropy	
	b. Corporate Social Responsibility	
3.	Where does charity come into it?	29
4.	Why Social Enterprise Matters	39
	a. Wealth Creation	
	b. Money leaks from communities	
	c. Empowering people	
	d. Avoiding grant-dependency	
	e. Positive effect on mainstream business	

5. Here be Dragons – Watch out!   43

6. Practicalities   49

    a. First Find your Social Entrepreneur
    b. When should you do it?
    c. How do you know it matters - Social Audit

7. Funding for a Social Enterprise   53

8. The Future   57

Appendix 1 Further Reading   61

Appendix 2 Definitions of Social Enterprise   63

Appendix 3 Cooperative Values and Principles   67

Appendix 4 Governance Structures for Social Enterprise 69

Appendix 5 Pros and Cons of various legal structures   73

Why this Book?

This book grew out of a series of workshops given to general business advisers to raise their awareness of Social Enterprise. These were intelligent people who were working with businesses, yet they had little or no knowledge of the so-called third sector.

From further market research, I have discovered that most people have no real idea of the size or scope of the not-for-profit sector or Social Enterprise, despite the fact that they come across organisations which are apparently Social Enterprises all the time.

Just to be clear, the first and second sectors of the economy are the private business sector, and Government - the public sector. The Third Sector includes all those organisations commonly referred to as non-profit or not-for-profit. It includes Charities, Social Enterprises, Community Businesses and other organisations set up for social purposes, rather than for generating profits for investors.

There are a number of books produced and aimed at people who work or volunteer in the Third Sector. This book is an attempt to demystify Social Enterprise for a general reader.

Why does Social Enterprise matter? It matters because it represents an alternative way of looking, on the one hand, at how business works and how it impacts society and, on the other, how social ends can be delivered differently from the traditional philanthropic charity model. It matters because politicians and the media have decided it could be an alternative way of providing public services

It mainly matters because there is a lot of it about. Most people are only dimly aware of it, if at all. And it could be important.

The problem lies in sorting out from the rhetoric, what Social Enterprise actually is, and what sort of benefit it can actually deliver.

Why a Second Edition?

Because people have been very kind in their reaction to the first edition and I was conscious of its imperfections.

But also Social Enterprise is a moving target and much has changed over the two years since the first edition was written.

There are now many more places for social enterprise to raise funds to realise their visions on changing the world, so the section financing has been extended..

I have also taken the opportunity of revising the advice on structures in the appendix.

Otherwise things are much as before.

1. What is Social Enterprise?

A lot of ink, not to say blood sweat and tears, has been shed in defining what Social Enterprise actually is. We have to start somewhere, and one of the least controversial is this definition from the UK Department of Trade and Industry:

> *Social Enterprises are businesses with primarily social objectives whose surpluses are principally reinvested for that purpose in the business or in the community, rather than being driven by the need to maximise profit for shareholders and owners.*

The key concepts here are:

- Business
- Use of surplus for a social benefit

Taking these in turn:

Social Enterprises are Businesses.

They trade. They buy and sell products or services. In traditional capitalist terms, they create wealth. Social Enterprise is "real" business

This emphasis on business is fundamental.

An organisation which relies in the long term on grant aid from the state or another funder or on donations from the general public for a significant part of its income cannot be said to be business, let alone a Social Enterprise.

It may be doing good things. It may be an excellent organisation, but it is not a business. It is not an enterprise.

This is not to say that the state has no role to play in helping a Social Enterprise in its start-up phase or if it is going through difficult trading conditions. The state provides start-up assistance to any businesses in particular geographical areas through various mechanisms via local authorities - Assisted Area status, European Block Grants, European Structural Fund support and so on. There are grants for training workforces or for creating or protecting jobs.

The UK Government has provided large amounts of money for the private sector in order to maintain key areas of the national or regional economy. The private car industry in the West Midlands, for example, received large payments in the late twentieth century. Similarly there are considerable incentives in setting up private businesses in the post-industrial areas of the UK, particularly the old mining and steel-producing areas.

Support for Social Enterprise should be on the same terms as if it were a "normal" business, for exactly the same reasons – that jobs are being created or safeguarded – that the economy is being boosted or protected.

Social Enterprises make a surplus to be reinvested for a social benefit.

For any organisation to continue in existence, it must take in more money each year than it pays out. It must follow Mr Micawber in Charles Dickens's novel "David Copperfield":

> *Annual income twenty pounds, annual expenditure nineteen nineteen six, result happiness. Annual income twenty pounds, annual expenditure twenty pounds ought and six, result misery.*

The difference between income and expenditure need not be large, but it must be there.

A friend of mine, when giving presentations on Social Enterprise to public sector workers has been known to make his audience chant in unison, the mantra: "Profit is good. Profit is good."

This is where we come across the first of many ideological challenges. There are some on the extreme **social** end of the spectrum who abhor the word **profit**, just as there are those at the other **enterprise** end who feel **surplus** is mealy-mouthed.

In the same way **not-for-profit** and **non-profit** do not mean that an organisation makes no profit - it would not survive for long without one - it is about why those profits are generated and how they are used.

The way in which a Social Enterprise reinvests its surplus may not be obvious immediately.

It may be that there are no shareholders to be paid back, although there may be other forms of borrowing. However, many Social Enterprises reinvest socially in more subtle ways. They may:

- **Employ people who are not attractive to other employers**
  - o People with disabilities
  - o Ex-offenders
  - o Mental health service users
  - o Those with few educational qualifications.

- **Operate in places which are not attractive to other businesses**
  - o Areas with low educational attainment
  - o Social housing estates
  - o Post-industrial areas
  - o Sparsely-populated rural areas

- **Operate in activities which have lower profit margins than would be acceptable to the private sector**
  - o The care sector, particularly looking after people in their own homes.

- **Operate in activities for ideological reasons**
  - o Renewable energy
  - o Recycling
  - o Fair Trade with the developing world.

Social Enterprise may benefit a specific community, although the definition of a community can be very broad:

- people who live in this area / town / valley / building /housing estate
- people of a specific ethnicity
- people with a particular disability
- people with a particular disadvantage such as mental health service users or recovering drug users.

Social Enterprises are accountable to stakeholders other than shareholders. They may for example have a membership structure as a cooperative in which all decisions are made by the members. They may have a Board of Directors drawn from the community they serve. They may be owned by the workers. They may be a charity accountable to the Charity Commission, providing benefit to the wider public.

Although a Social Enterprise may have a leading figure to drive it, sometimes called a **Social Entrepreneur,** it requires the backing and hard work of a number of other people.

It is difficult, perhaps impossible, to be a Social Enterprise on your own as an individual. This has implications for control of the enterprise, which usually rests with a group of people.

For this reason many entrepreneurs choose to set up a traditional for-profit company and then use the profits for social purposes. Andrew Carnegie in the nineteenth century and Bill Gates in the twenty-first are striking examples of this model of helping society. Neither could be said to have set up a Social Enterprise.

a. A Quiz – What are these entities? Are they Social Enterprises?

1. The Arts Council of England
2. English National Opera
3. The Welsh Rugby Union
4. The Lawn Tennis Association
5. Glamorgan and Gwent Housing Association
6. The National Museum and Galleries of Wales
7. The Institute of Grassland and Environmental Research
8. Harrow School
9. BUPA
10. Welsh Joint Education Committee
11. Amnesty International
12. Greenpeace
13. Oxfam
14. Network Rail
15. Glas Cymru – parent company of Welsh Water plc

Are they companies, charities, not for profit organisations?

Don't worry if you have no idea. My experience is that most people have given no thought to the governance or accountability of many of the organisations they encounter on a daily basis.

You can also ponder this simple question:

What is the largest charity by annual turnover in England and Wales?

Most people have only a fuzzy idea what a charity is.

People automatically start to enumerate the twenty largest charities which ask the general public for funds. The largest of these is Cancer Research UK, which is a long way behind the largest charity by assets – medical research charity, The Wellcome Trust. The sheer number of charities on the register for England and Wales is also a surprise – 180,000 – 167,000 if you take out those which are not independent. Then there are all the charities in Scotland and Northern Ireland as well.

I have yet to find anyone, even someone in the "trade", to tell me that the **Arts Council of England** is the largest charity by income in England, just as the **Arts Council of Wales** is the largest charity by income with a head office in Wales. Their income comes from Government or from money generated from the National Lottery. The Trustees of the Arts Council are appointed by Government, but they operate independently under charity law, as the National Assembly for Wales found out in 2006 when it tried to annex the Arts Council of Wales into the Government.

There is no such thing as a non-profit organisation under UK law. The nearest to it is a Company limited by Guarantee or the Community Interest Companies which started being registered in late 2005. More later about precisely what these are.

Let's go back to some more of the organisations on the list. More of them are charities than many people expect. Many of them are also Companies limited by Guarantee – not distributing funds to shareholders.

English National Opera, like **Welsh National Opera,** is a company limited by guarantee and also a registered charity. Many arts organisations are set up like this.

Sports bodies such as England's **Rugby Football Union**, or the **Welsh Rugby Union** or the **Lawn Tennis Association** are generally Companies limited by Guarantee. They often have associated charities which encourage the use of the game among the disadvantaged, and into which profits can be moved tax-effectively. They are membership organisations owned and controlled by their members.

Glamorgan and Gwent Housing Association is an Industrial and Provident Association, as are many of the housing associations which are becoming the major providers of social housing in England and Wales. Much of the social housing which was in local council control is being gradually transferred to housing associations. Usually this is to a Social Enterprise set up specifically for the purpose like Valleys to Coast, which has taken over all the housing stock from Bridgend County Borough Council in South Wales. By historical quirk Industrial and Provident Societies are not administered by Companies House or the Charity Commission, but the Financial Services Authority. This is presumably because the large mutual Building Societies like the Nationwide share this structure, and it is felt they should be regulated by the organisation which deals with banks.

The National Museum and Galleries of Wales like many museums, local and national, is a company limited by guarantee which is a registered charity.

The Institute of Grassland and Environmental Research went by the more evocative name of the Welsh Plant Breeding Station when I was at university in Aberystwyth nearby on the far west coast. It was a government research institute under the auspices of the Agricultural Research Council in the 1980's when it was set free to act commercially. It is now one of Wales's largest charities with a strong commercial remit, providing grass varieties suitable for Wimbledon and Wembley Stadium, as well as for agricultural use throughout the world. Since the first edition of this book, IGER has merged with another charity, Aberystwyth University. Most Universities are also charities, registered with the Charity Commission or regulated under Government Statute.

Harrow School like many of the public schools including Eton was set up to educate the poor. It may be one of the most elite private schools commanding high fees from wealthy parents, but it is a charity registered with Charity Commission, as are most independent schools.

This is because education was considered of its nature to be a charitable activity up until the passing of the 2006 Charities Act, which decrees that public benefit must come into it as well. The Charity Commission is interpreting public benefit at least in part by how many scholarships are offered to those whose parent cannot afford fees.

BUPA is well known as one of the leading suppliers of private medicine in the UK and worldwide and with its aggressive marketing gives every appearance of being a commercial company. The initials stand for British United Provident Association. It is a mutual organisation, a company limited by guarantee owned by its members who are its customers. Profits are ploughed back into the business or passed to an associated medical charity.

Welsh Joint Education Committee is the examination body which provides GCSE's, A-levels and other qualifications for schools in Wales, in the wider UK, and around the world. Surprisingly, it is a company limited by guarantee as well as being a registered charity. Board members are appointed by local education authorities in Wales.

Most people assume that **Amnesty International** and **Greenpeace** are charities. In fact they are both companies limited by guarantee and are not allowed to be charities because of their overt political stance. Political organisations including political parties cannot be charities. Of course Amnesty has an associated charity which provides practical aid to prisoners of conscience, but that is separate from its main activity. As a rule of thumb, you can tell whether an organisation is charitable, if, when you make a donation, they ask you to sign a Gift Aid declaration so that the charity can claim back the income tax you have paid on your donation.

Oxfam is one of the largest charities collecting funds from the general public. It is a company limited by guarantee and registered with the Charity Commission. However, the shops marked Oxfam you see on the High Street are actually operated by a subsidiary company which gifts its profits to Oxfam. Charity Company subsidiaries are a common method of getting around the restrictions on trading for charities. Oxfam's trading subsidiaries are clearly Social Enterprises which have been very successful financially for Oxfam, which was one of the first major recyclers in the UK before it was fashionable and is now the largest second hand bookseller in Europe, shifting more than 11 million books per annum.

Glas Cymru – parent company of Welsh Water plc is arguably the largest Social Enterprise with a head office in Wales. When Hyder, the parent company of Welsh Water, the water and sewerage utility, got into financial difficulties in the 1990's, Glas Cymru was formed as a company limited by guarantee to take over its assets. It has no shareholders, and a board which is appointed to be representative of the people of Wales. All profits are used within the company. The other large water companies in the UK are private businesses with shareholders. **Network Rail** was formed using this model following the collapse of Railtrack to take over the UK's rail infrastructure. It is a company limited by guarantee with all profits reinvested in the UK's railways.

****

The purpose of this section is to show the wide variety and size of organisations which could be termed Social Enterprises. I leave it to the reader to form an opinion as to whether they are or are not. They all meet the Department of Trade and Industry definition, but many of them may not consider themselves part of the Social Enterprise industry.

There is an assumption in some quarters that Social Enterprise equates to small earnest well-meaning, but ultimately ineffectual organisations, struggling to do good things. As you can see, this is not actually the case.

9

b. Social Enterprise is not new

The use of Social Enterprise as a term is relatively recent. It was first used in the UK parliament in the early nineteen-nineties. However, the concept of using business methods for social ends has been going on for centuries.

The monasteries run in the United Kingdom by the Catholic Church until their assets were confiscated by King Henry VIII are a good example. They owned lands and were responsible for the livelihood of large numbers of people who worked on their farms and industries. Profits helped to pay for the upkeep of their religious life.

There are several possible business models for a Social Enterprise:

- A stand alone company with social aims

- A charity which charges for its services (but not one which depends solely on grant or philanthropic income)

- A trading subsidiary of a charity

- A mutual organisation owned by its members or customers.

This can mean creating a business which unites its business aims with its mission like the highly successful **Big Issue** street newspaper sold by homeless vendors throughout the UK, set up in 1991. Big Issue publishes and wholesales a magazine, which is purchased by homeless people who retail it to the general public.

Each vendor is running a retail business. They pay half the cover price to Big Issue up front; no credit allowed; no returns. Big Issue pays its profit to the Big Issue Foundation which is a charity working with street homeless. The vendors spend their profit on eating, living and re-establishing their lives.

The socially linked businesses most visible to the general public are the charity shops on UK High Streets, selling donated goods, but sometimes also goods related to the charity's main purpose. Contrary to what you may think, many charity shops are not actually trading as businesses. Those which only sell donated goods are actually part of a fundraising operation. They are converting one form of donation – used clothes – into another form – money. As soon as goods are being bought in for sale then trading is occurring as far as the tax authorities are concerned, and many charities operate their shops through separate trading activities.

A good example is **Oxfam UK** which "works with others to overcome poverty and suffering" It operates its UK chain of charity shops partnership through a trading subsidiary which buys and sells Fair-Trade goods made in the developing world., as well as being one of the largest recyclers in the UK. Oxfam was into recycling long before it was fashionable.

Oxfam's shops opened for business in 1948, but the **Red Cross** had about 150 shops during the Second World War from 1941, repeating the success of its bazaar at Shepherd's Market in London during the First World War.

Trading subsidiaries can also be in totally unrelated businesses. **Cardiff YMCA,** a registered charity which was founded in the mid nineteenth century provides training and support for young vulnerable people. It has an associated Housing Association which manages board and lodge hostels for homeless and vulnerable young people. Its very successful trading subsidiary is called Green Willow Funerals Ltd which has funeral homes in Cardiff, Newport and a head office in the Vale of Glamorgan.

Mencap, the large UK learning disability charity, set up a successful insurance company in the 1990's specializing in insurance for charities and people with disabilities; a customer-base ill-served by commercial insurance companies at the time. The finance director of the charity had moved from a senior position in a large insurance company and saw a niche. MCIS now trades independently, but still donates profits to Mencap.

The Salvation Army got into Social Enterprise even earlier in 1890 when its founder General William Booth established what was known as The Salvation Army Bank. It now trades as Reliance Bank Limited and has, to quote its own publicity material "built upon caring foundations - that remain as strong as ever." The Salvation Army Trustee Company and The Salvation Army International Trustee Company still retain sole ownership of the bank and each year receive an equal share of the Bank's allowable profits which are used to further The Salvation Army's evangelical and charitable work.

The National Trust was founded in 1895 by three Victorian philanthropists - Miss Octavia Hill, Sir Robert Hunter and Canon Hardwicke Rawnsley. Concerned about the impact of uncontrolled development and industrialisation, they set up the Trust to act as a guardian for the nation in the acquisition and protection of threatened coastline, countryside and buildings in the UK.

The National Trust, a registered charity, now looks after 248,000 hectares (612,000 acres) of beautiful countryside in England, Wales and Northern Ireland, plus more than 700 miles of coastline and more than 200 buildings and gardens of outstanding interest and importance.

It has 3.4 million members whose subscriptions form a significant part of its income, but trading is also important. It charges for entry to many of its sites, has a chain of shops, both at its own properties, and in the High Streets of the UK. It also lets out holiday cottages and has financial arrangements with travel companies.

I doubt whether the **Public School** system in the UK considers itself as part of the social economy. (For those outside the UK, Public School means private education; sometimes very expensive private education.) It may surprise you to know that most of the private schools in Britain are charities, and despite the best efforts of many left-wing Labour MPs over the years still attract all the tax benefits that go with that.

Public Schools are businesses which charge parents to provide education for their offspring and then reinvest the proceeds in scholarships for those who are deserving, but cannot afford the fees.

Harrow School was founded in 1572 under the Royal Charter granted by Elizabeth I to John Lyon, a local farmer. The underlying charity is

called: *The Keepers and Governors of the Free Grammar School of John Lyon.*
and in 1872 because it had moved so far from its original roots, it set
up John Lyon School to educate local pupils. **Eton College** is even
older. It was founded in 1440 by Henry VI, founded as 'The King's
College of Our Lady of Eton beside Windsor' with provision made for
70 scholars to receive free education.

The **Cooperative movement** is another well-known manifestation of
Social Enterprise. It dates its foundation to the Rochdale Equitable
Pioneers Society set up 1844 by a group of 28 artisans working in the
cotton mills in the town of Rochdale, in the north of England, but was
prefigured by Robert Owen from Newtown in mid-Wales who set up
his ideal village of New Lanark in Scotland in the late eighteenth
century. This led to a nationwide chain of cooperative grocery shops
which flourished throughout the UK in the twentieth century and into
the twenty-first, the Cooperative Wholesale Society and the very
successful Cooperative Bank. More about cooperatives later.

c. Using the right words

Social Enterprises tend to be based around strong values. A good demonstration of this is **One Village** in Oxfordshire, a retailer and wholesaler of "craft-made functional articles for the home: rugs and floormats, cushions, lampshades, duvet covers, throws and textiles, home accessories and crockery, baskets and containers....."

This is taken from the front page of their web site www.onevillage.org

> *All this selling is a service. A service of course to customers, who enjoy the products as useful articles for the home. But also, and actually more importantly, a service for the producers of these articles – craftmakers in some of the poorest parts of the world.* **One Village** *was set up for their benefit: to build up communities, to stand alongside others in the struggle towards a more equitable and just world order.*

And further into the web site

> *Long before people thought up the slogan "fair trade", One Village was one of the pioneers of marketing for social change when, in 1979, we set out as marketing support for craftmakers' cooperatives. The first priority of One Village remains support to artisans' coops, although we achieve this by providing customers with exceptional products that cannot easily be found elsewhere.*

They also publish their operating principles on the web site. Customers are important, but the purpose of the organisation is much more than that. Customers are changing the world, not just investing in home furnishing. There is almost a sense in which they would like to deal only with the "right" customers who share their values..

I particularly like point 10 of their "operating methodology"

> *Products are sold in ways which honour producers and customers, and which enhance public appreciation of the craft, and of the skill and humanity of the producers.*

It is important to separate the different **philosophical** foundation of a Social Enterprise from its **legal** governance structure.

Legal structures

These are the legal governance structures which are available to a Social Enterprise:

- Unincorporated association
- Charitable trust
- Company limited by guarantee
- Industrial and Provident society

The first three can become **charities** registered with the Charity Commission, and coming within its legal regulation.

An Industrial and Provident society can be designated as having charitable purposes, and can be registered with Her Majesty's Revenue and Customes as an **exempt** charity in order to receive the tax benefits of charitable status.

Charity law was revised by Parliament in the Charities Act 2006, the first major overhaul for some four centuries. It suggested a new corporate entity – the **Charitable Incorporated Organisation** (CIO) originally scheduled for 2008, but not now expected until some time in 2010. This will simplify the need for charities which are also companies limited by guarantee to have to send two sets of accounts in different formats to the Charity Commission and Companies House.

Finally the **Community Interest Company** (CIC) was introduced in late 2005 as a vehicle for Social Enterprises. CIC's cannot be charitable, but they have an asset lock which protects the organisation's assets. They come under the Community Interest Regulator at Companies House. CIC's can be companies limited by guarantee or they can have shareholders whose dividends are capped. If they are large enough it is possible for a CIC to be a public limited company.

More details about these entities are given in an Appendix, and the pros and cons are considered in chapter 5 on the practicalities of setting up a Social Enterprise.

Philosophical structures

These terms relate to how the organisation sees itself. All can be termed Social Enterprises, and there are Social Enterprises which do not fall into any of these particular categories.

- Social Firm
- Development Trust
- Community Enterprise
- Cooperative
- Credit Union

There are examples of each philosophical structure constituted as each of the legal structures, with or without charitable status. They also overlap. Community Cooperatives may be Community Enterprises as may Development Trusts. It may depend on whom one is talking to.

Social Firms

The Social Firm movement grew up from the desire to provide genuine paid employment for people with disabilities, where they could work with people with no disability and be treated with the dignity and respect they deserve. In the jargon of disability the key words are integration and empowerment.

The traditional model was the manufacturing workshop which employed only disabled people – blind people making brushes, basket weaving, and so on. The large number of factories set up by Remploy after the second Wold War, some of which are still operating, were examples of this. As manufacturing in the UK has declined, Remploy has moved into service industries, and now its main emphasis is on placing disabled people in regular businesses, with good support.

The old manufacturing model relied heavily of government subsidy, and had a tendency to form disabled people ghettos, something which the Social Firm movement would discourage.

The concept of a Social Firm has been broadened to encompass a wider range of disadvantaged people as well as those conventionally described as disabled, for example, mental health service users, those recovering from drug abuse and homeless people.

Under the Social Firms UK definition at least twenty-five per cent of the employees of a Social Firm should be disadvantaged.

There is significant pressure on the Social Services Departments of local authorities in the UK to develop Social Firms as a partial replacement of their day centre provision.   Crudely put, this is to give the disabled people something more useful to do than just occupying them and giving carers a respite.

An excellent example is the **Pack-It Group** in Cardiff, which was established in 1988 to provide training opportunities and permanent paid employment for people with learning disabilities. It has grown from its early beginnings to a three pronged business supplying mailing, storage & distribution and on-line fulfilment.

Pack-It started as a project within South Glamorgan County Council's Social Services Department in a shed on the old East Moors Steelworks site. It moved to a new unit at the Cardiff Bay Business Park in 1998, with a loan from the Industrial Common Ownership Fund. Within two years it had four units, and now operates from the largest warehouse on the site. It makes a profit on a turnover of £1.5 million, with no grant support.

Pack-It has an impressive range of clients, many in the public sector. Contracts are bid for competitively in the normal way. Clients include the Welsh Assembly Government, Jazz News, Western Mail and Echo, many of the Chambers of Commerce in Wales, Rockwool and The Institute of Welsh Affairs.

More at www.pack-it.co.uk. The Social Firms UK website is www.socialfirms.co.uk

Community Enterprise

A community enterprise is a Social Enterprise based around a community. This can be a geographical community or a community of interest – those in a particular ethnic group, with a shared disability or with a particular affinity.

The most usual model is based around a particular geographical area, often focussed on a building - the village school which closes through declining pupil numbers, the local Workmen's Institute, the local post office.

A typical example is **Cwmaman Institute**, based in a small former mining village near Aberdare in Rhondda Cynon Taf , a community which had high unemployment levels, and almost half its population with no access to a car. The Institute was built in 1892, paid for by the local community. By the early 1990's it had fallen into disrepair, and was eventually rebuilt with grant funding from the Arts Council for Wales, the European Union and the Coalfields Regeneration Trust, locally raised funds, topped up with a loan from the Cooperative Bank.

As well as the main auditorium, it now has two bars, an outside courtyard that can be used for special events, a skittle alley, a fitness suite, a state of the art cinema, and a variety of multipurpose rooms that are available for hire to nearly forty local organisations like the award-winning Cwmaman Silver Band.

Turnover is now over £500,000 per year, which covers its operating costs. Twenty-four full time equivalent jobs have been created and eighty local volunteers help out on a regular basis.

More at www.cwmamaninstitute.co.uk

An instanceof a community defined by ethnicity is the **Swansea Chinese Community Coop Centre**, which was set up in 1996 by a group of enthusiastic volunteers. It has 400 members throughout South Wales, though predominantly in Swansea and its immediate area. Its aims are:

> *To assist the Chinese people to obtain their entitled welfare and benefits; to provide leisure activities; to promote Chinese traditions and culture; to advocate social harmony and to advance peaceful and friendly relationship between Chinese and other ethnic groups and to organise educational and cultural events.*

The Centre targets women, the youth and the elderly and services range from interpretation/translation, training courses, talks & seminars, cultural & hobby classes, day & short trips and social and cultural events such as the annual Chinese New Year celebrations.

More at www.swanseachinese.co.uk

Development Trusts

The Development Trusts Association defines a development trust as an organisation which is:

- community based, owned and led

- engaged in the economic, environmental and social regeneration of a defined area or community

- independent but seeking to work in partnership with other private, voluntary and public sector organisations

- self-sufficient or aiming for self sufficiency, and not for private profit.

Development Trusts are particularly focussed on the use of community-owned assets for regeneration. Community-owned assets can be used to raise finance to put into practice their community activities.

A particularly good example of what can be done is **Cwmni Tref Caernarfon** (now **Galeri Caernarfon Cyf**) in the North West corner of Wales. Its aims are:

> *To pursue social, economic and environmental projects for the benefit of the community in Caernarfon and its environs.*

Caernarfon, despite having one of the most stunning and well-preserved castles in the UK, with large numbers of tourist visitors from around the world, was by 1990 very run down and neglected with many empty and derelict properties in the town centre. Cwmni Tref was set up in 1992 to do something about this. With a grant from the Welsh Development Agency, they bought and renovated a property. They let out the building for commercial use and used the income to raise loans to buy a second property, then a third and so on. They currently have twenty properties in the town centre which were formerly derelict and are now thriving businesses.

One of the board's dreams was to create an enterprise centre to regenerate the town, and Galeri was opened in 2005. It houses a four hundred-seat theatre, two large rehearsal studios, an art space, café bar, rooms for hire and 27 enterprise units, let to businesses in the creative sector.

The latest project is to carry on the work in the former slate mining valleys of Ogwen, Peris, Nantlle, Ffestiniog and Corris. This is being done through a new company called Cwmni Adwy, which since 2000 has renovated eleven properties for rent as workspaces or offices.

Cwmni Tref's work has changed the face of the Caernarfon, to quote Gwyn Roberts, its Chief Executive:

> *'It doesn't bear much resemblance to a town where ten years ago you couldn't give commercial leases away and there was no proper venue for cultural and artistic events. Today we don't really have any trouble letting the 40 shops, offices and flats we have bought and refurbished. What's more, our success has encouraged the private sector to bring other empty properties back into use. Our efforts have made a great contribution to improving the economic and social wellbeing of the town'.*

More at www.galericaernarfon.com and www.cwmniadwy.co.uk

Cooperatives

Cooperatives are a particular sort of Social Enterprise with a well-defined set of values and democratic principles, a long heritage based around the cooperative movement worldwide.

The Cooperative Movement dates its foundation to the Rochdale Equitable Pioneers Society set up 1844 by a group of 28 artisans working in the cotton mills in the town of Rochdale, in the north of England. Working conditions were poor, and wages low, and they decided that by pooling what little they had, they could access basic goods at lower prices. This idea grew into a chain of shops and associated businesses in which customers were also members who shared in the overall profits – the Cooperative Dividend.

The Cooperative Movement world-wide regularly reviews the definition of a cooperative and its statement of values and principles. The latest 1995 version is given below. A fuller version is in Appendix 3.

> *A cooperative is defined as an autonomous association of persons united voluntarily to meet their common economic, social, and cultural needs and aspirations through a jointly-owned and democratically controlled enterprise.*

Values:

- self-help
- self-responsibility
- democracy
- equality
- equity
- solidarity

Principles:

1. Voluntary and Open Membership

2. Democratic Member Control

3. Member Economic Participation

4. Autonomy and Independence

5. Education, Training and Information

6. Cooperation among Cooperatives

7. Concern for Community

Broadly in the UK cooperatives are:

- Worker Cooperatives
- Community Cooperatives
- Secondary Cooperatives
- Credit Unions

It has to be emphasised that a cooperative is a state of mind and a way of operating. A cooperative can be an Industrial and Provident society, but it may be an ordinary Company Limited by Guarantee or a Community Interest Company, in each case with cooperative principles built into its memorandum and articles.

Worker Cooperatives

Workers cooperatives are enterprises wholly owned and managed by their workers. Sometimes they are set up from scratch, but often they come into being when an entrepreneur who set up a company decides to sell out, and the workers are in position to buy the business, or a crisis develops and the employees take over the business to save it..

An example of the latter is Tower Colliery near Aberdare in the South Wales coalfield which was closed by British Coal in 1994. The deep mine had been in existence since the mid nineteenth century and the miners who worked there formed a cooperative company, bought it and ran it successfully, selling to the industrial and domestic market, until its final closure in January 2008.

Scott Bader Ltd , world-wide polymer company based in Wollaston, Northamptonshire UK set up in 1921 was transferred in 1951 to its workforce. Each employee joins and subscribes to the spirit of Scott Bader:

Everyone working in Scott Bader is expected to become a member of the Scott Bader Commonwealth. Members share the responsibilities and privileges of being trustees-in-common and working the Scott Bader way, and must accept the challenge of ensuring the company is sustainable for the benefit of future generations.

Community Cooperatives

Community buildings can be set up on a cooperative model by the local community rather than as a charity or community interest company model.

An example of this is Noddfa Chapel in Maesteg, South Wales. The community decided to take on the renovation of a redundant chapel for the community and now it is run as a community facility with each member of the community having a say in what can take place there.

Another community cooperative is that created by the residents of the Tre Cwm Estate in Llandudno who built their own new community centre which opened in 2003 to revitalise the area. It now provides training courses, youth clubs, pensioners' luncheon club, mother & toddler group, homework club, sporting activities and a job club.

Secondary Cooperatives

Secondary Cooperatives tend to be set up by groups of businesses as membership organisations for mutual benefit. For example, Welsh Lamb And Beef Promotions Limited is owned by Welsh farmers and promotes and markets meat products.

Carmarthen and Pumpsaint Farmers Limited, of which my father was a member when I was growing up on a hill farm in West Wales is a buying consortium. Members can buy livestock feedstuff and other agricultural products more cheaply than from private companies – a great help to hard-pressed farmers.

Credit Unions

To quote ABCUL the umbrella body for Credit Unions in the UK:

> *Credit unions are financial cooperatives owned and controlled by their members. They offer savings and great value loans plus they are local, ethical and know what their members want. Each credit union has a "common bond" which determines who can join it. The common bond may be for people living or working in the same area, people working for the same employer or people who belong to the same association, such as a church or trade union.*

Credit unions are particularly popular in the US, Ireland, Canada and Australia, but were relatively late to start in the UK. The Credit Union Act 1979 created a proper legal structure for the first time.

In the UK, they are particularly associated with those on lower incomes who may have trouble managing their money, and who are not particularly welcomed by the commercial banking system. They are a particularly powerful way of avoiding the high interest rates of loan sharks.

More at www.abcul.org

2. Not Social Enterprise

Just as important as defining Social Enterprise is looking at organisations that might look like Social Enterprise, but are definitely not.

There have always been **philanthropists** who make their money from business and then use it for social ends. Andrew Carnegie in the nineteenth century created a hugely successful steel business and then gave away a large proportion of the profits. He provided funds for over 2,500 public libraries in the United Kingdom, the United States, Australia and other countries.

A modern counterpart is Bill Gates, founder of Microsoft who is using a proportion of his huge wealth to combat AIDS in the Developing World.

This use of money generated by "normal" business for good work cannot really be termed Social Enterprise. This is not to denigrate the motives of those involved. However, the purpose of Microsoft is not to make money for philanthropy. It exists mainly to provide profits for its investors.

A common mechanism, usually to take advantage of tax laws, is to use associated charitable foundations which are at arms length from the business, and receive some of the profits. The Bill and Melinda Gates Foundation accepts large donations from the money generated from Bill Gates' share of Microsoft.

Some companies have formal links to their associated charity. For example Lloyds-TSB Bank donates one per cent of its profits to the Lloyds-TSB Foundation. This is enshrined in its governance, as a legacy of the merger of Lloyds Bank with the Trustee Saving Bank. TSB was a mutual organisation – effectively a Social Enterprise owned by its members – and it gave one per cent of its profits for social ends via a charitable trust. Lloyds-TSB Foundation is a result of the terms of the merger.

Nationwide Building Society, the last of the big mutual building societies – a Social Enterprise? – has an associated foundation which will benefit hugely if Nationwide should demutualise and become a public company. Shares which would go to newer members will go to the Foundation if that happens.

A recent trend is the idea of **venture philanthropy**. This is where the philanthropist aims to follow the use of the money. For example, a gift is given to a charity on condition that the philanthropist has a seat on the Board of Trustees. This is particularly popular with new technology millionaires, but philanthropists throughout the ages have always been keen to ensure that their money is being used wisely.

There are examples of private, conventional, capitalist businesses with strong ethical standpoints, which may well use their social conscience as a selling point.

Body Shop built up a very strong brand based on natural ingredients, not using animal testing and sourcing products from the less-developed parts of the world. The sales proposition is that the world is a better place because you buy cosmetics at Body Shop. Body Shop has a strong social conscience and has many of the values of Social Enterprise, but ultimately profits go to shareholders who are being rewarded for risking their money investing in a cosmetic company. They were rewarded when the company was taken over by L'Oreal in 2006.

This mainstreaming of socially aware private enterprise is a constant source of concern for ethically aware shoppers. Is it still permissible to buy Ben and Jerry Ice Cream now they are part of Unilever? Ben and Jerry have a good record of opening franchises owned by Social Enterprises in the US and in the UK. Is that enough? Does their fair-trade vanilla ice cream count?

Further muddying the waters is the idea of **Corporate Social Responsibility (CSR).** This is the concept that organizations, especially companies, have an obligation to consider the interests of customers, employees, shareholders, communities, and environmental

26

considerations in all aspects of their operations. This obligation is seen to extend beyond their statutory obligation to comply with legislation.

Most big companies devote some of their web sites and annual reports to CSR. How well this is integrated into their actual day to day operations may be questionable. For example, BAE Systems which designs and manufactures arms for the world's more belligerent governments produce an annual report on their CSR which, among other items, considers the use of lead-free bullets which are less polluting when battlefields are cleared up after conflicts.

Increasingly companies see a strong ethical or environmental stance as a useful commercial opportunity. Consider how environmentally friendly all the major oil companies are in their corporate advertising.

This use of a strong ethical standpoint as a commercial advantage is the Cooperative Bank - a Social Enterprise. I remember being surprised when opening a business bank account to be asked to tick a yes / no box answering the question – Do you make chemical weapons? and another: Do you make instruments of torture? I suspect that chemical warfare manufacturers are not natural clients of the Cooperative Bank, but they can truthfully make some strong statements in advertising about the sort of customers they have. I suspect that none of the other banks has asked all its clients either question.

3. Where does Charity come into it?

Many Social Enterprises are charities, because of their social remit, so it is important to be clear what a charity is. It is also important to remember that most charities are not Social Enterprises. Most charities depend on the support of donors, who give money or other resources to enable them to perform their charitable activities. Trading is not a charitable activity.

The foundations for modern charity were laid down in the Charitable Uses Act of 1601 by Queen Elizabeth I. They were reviewed as part of what is known as the Pemsel Case by Lord Macnaghten in 1891. He restated the four **Heads of Charity** which, until the 2006 Charities Act, formed the basis of deciding whether an activity was charitable. These are:

- Relief of poverty
- Advancement of education
- Advancement of religion
- Other purposes beneficial to the community.

The 2006 Charities Act was the first attempt for four centuries to redefine what is charitable. The Act defined twelve **charitable purposes** and a catch-all general heading:

- the prevention or relief of poverty
- the advancement of education
- the advancement of religion
- the advancement of health or the saving of lives
- the advancement of citizenship or community development
- the advancement of the arts, culture, heritage or science
- the advancement of amateur sport
- the advancement of human rights, conflict resolution or reconciliation or the promotion of religious or racial harmony or equality and diversity

- the advancement of environmental protection or improvement
- the relief of those in need by reason of youth, age, ill-health, disability, financial hardship or other disadvantage
- the advancement of animal welfare
- the promotion of the efficiency of the armed forces of the Crown; or the efficiency of the police, fire and rescue services or ambulance services,
- any other purposes charitable in law.

These are charitable purposes if they are carried out for the public benefit. Public benefit is not actually defined in the Act. Essentially, it is what a reasonable person would say is a public benefit. Undoubtedly this will be tested in the courts to get clearer definition.

The basis of charity law is the relationship between three parties:

- Donors
- Trustees
- Beneficiaries

Donors give money, time or resources. The trustees' role is to ensure that the donors' wishes are carried out to the benefit of the beneficiaries. This sets up a 'Trust', hence the name 'Trustee'. The trustees can either carry out the trust themselves or can delegate it to volunteers or employees.

Betraying their Elizabethan origins, charities have **Objects** and **Powers** which are enshrined within their governing documents. None of your new-fangled aims and objectives.

Objects describe what the charity was set up to do – to save the whale; to provide a community centre in a village to be used by the general public. **Powers** explain what it is allowed to do in furtherance of the object – to employ people, to own property, to enter into contracts, to raise funds. Charities sometimes come unstuck when they extend their activities without looking back at their governing document which says what they can or cannot do. For example, it may be difficult to become a Social Enterprise if the organization has no power to charge for good and services.

Most charities in England and Wales are registered with the Charity Commission. There are also what is known as exempt and excepted charities, many of which are also coming under the Charity Commission's regulation under the 2006 Charities Act. Northern Ireland and Scotland have separate regulations.

There are over 167,000 independent registered charities in England and Wales. However, most of them are very small, as can be seen from the table below.

No income or no recorded income	9,248	5.5%
£1 to £10k	81,774	48.8%
£10k to £25k	27,430	16.4%
£25k to £100k	25,103	15.0%
£100k to £250k	10,451	6.2%
£250k to £1m	8,321	5.0%
£1m to £5m	3,721	2.2%
£5m to £10m	687	0.4%
£10m to £25m	447	0.3%
Over £25m	223	0.1%
TOTAL	**167,405**	**100.0%**

Source: Guidestar UK Jul 2006

Some of the smaller charities may now be defunct. The Charity Commission with new powers under the 2006 Charities Act has started on what is essentially a cull. If charities do not respond to correspondence they will be removed from the register. The lower limit for registration is also being raised to £5,000.

According to the Charity Commission:

A body is a charity if it is:

- *Set up under the law of England and Wales; and*

- *Is established for exclusively charitable purposes*

To be a charity an organisation must have purposes that are exclusively charitable. A charity's purposes are its objects or aims, which are usually set out in its governing document. The meaning of "charitable purposes" is largely based upon the decisions of the Court and the Charity Commission over the years. Generally, if an organisation is a charity then it must apply to the Commission for registration, and the Commission must register it.

Many Social Enterprises are eligible to become charities because of their social remit.

Trading by charities is not in itself a charitable activity. Nonetheless many charities do trade. Trading by charities is either primary or secondary.

- **Primary** purpose trading is trading in direct furtherance of the charity's objects: a disability charity providing a service for people with visual impairments under contract to the local council, or publishing books for architects on designing buildings friendly to the visually impaired. Primary trading does not incur corporation tax.

- **Secondary** purpose trading is an activity which is unrelated to the purpose of the charity. Cardiff YMCA's funeral director subsidiary would be a classic example. A charity is allowed to profit from an unrelated business activity only up at a certain level, before the activity is classed as a business which must be taxed just as any other would be. Usually, a charity will create a trading subsidiary, which will then pass its profits back to the charity and thus avoid paying corporation tax. This is what Cardiff YMCA does.

A further complication is **ancillary trading**. A theatre which is a charity can sell tickets for performances because it is within its primary purpose. It is expected that a theatre will have a bar which is open for sale of drinks, sweets and ice cream before a performance, at the interval and after the show. This is ancillary trading. If, however, the bar is open at times other than when a performance is taking place, this may become secondary trading. Is this a theatre with a café attached or a café with a built-in theatre?

The Victoria and Albert Museum in London used to advertise itself as a good restaurant with a museum attached. One hopes that they had the café safely run by a trading subsidiary rather than directly by the charity.

One common misconception is that Charities are exempt from Value Added Tax (VAT). This is not the case, although there are some concessions for fundraising activities, like printing fundraising material. Most charities which do not trade have large irrecoverable VAT bills because they cannot reclaim VAT on their non-trading activities.

The legal structures for a charity are:

- **Unincorporated association.** This is how most charities start - a few people round a kitchen table with an urge to do something which will improve society. A constitution is drawn up with mechanisms for a membership and how to elect chair, secretary, treasurer and so on.

- **Charitable trust.** This is where a small group of people, perhaps half a dozen look after assets – money or a building – for wider benefit. Here the governing document is a trust deed. Trustees may not be elected by a membership, but have some other method of selection. Often this is simply the power to appoint someone agreed by all the remaining trustees.

- **Company limited by guarantee.** This is used when the trustees want to limit their liabilities. In the first two models, the trustees are personally liable for anything that goes wrong

33

with the charity. When the charity is incorporated as a company, then it exists in its own right and can enter into its own contracts which are not personally guaranteed by the Trustees. Charities often start as unincorporated organisations and then become incorporated when they get bigger and start to employ people or own substantial assets like buildings. One complication here is the need to send accounts to two regulators – the Charity Commission who are interested in whether the money is being spent for charity – and Companies House who want to know if the organisation is solvent and not breaking company law.

- **Charitable Incorporated Organisation.** This is a form set out in the 2006 Charities act which provides limited liability for trustees without setting up a company. The first CIOs are expected in mid 2010. They will only have to report to the Charity Commission, saving on accounting costs.

For the sake of completeness, I should mention two other forms of charity, neither of which is likely to be of much use to Social Enterprise - **exempted** and **excepted** charities. These are charities which do not come within the regulation of the Charity Commission. The Charities Act 2006 brings some of them into the fold. Examples here are some churches covered by the Places of Worship Registration Act of 1855, such as the Presbyterian Church of Wales. Others were registered for charitable purposes by Royal Charters or directly through Parliament. Several of the older universities are exempt charities.

One other possible structure for a charitable Social Enterprise is as an **Industrial and Provident Society with charitable aims.** Industrial and Provident Societies are regulated by the Financial Services Authority, which also looks after Credit Unions and mutual organisations such as Building Societies and insurance companies.

An industrial and provident society with charitable aims can register to receive Gift Aid from Her Majesty's Revenue and Customs, despite not being registered with the Charity Commission.

An example is Care and Repair Cymru, an organisation which helps older people to stay on in their own homes by providing specially adapted aids, or simple basic security items. It was set up by a group of housing associations, most of which were themselves Industrial and Provident Associations. They felt more comfortable with this structure and effectively set up a charity in their own image.

Some charities are Social Enterprises in their own right, because they obtain most if not all of their income from trading. However a more common way in which charities enter the realms of Social Enterprise is via **charity trading subsidiaries.** This is the route taken by Cardiff YMCA with its funeral business, and Oxfam with its shops.

Before a charity sets up a trading subsidiary, these are the considerations to take into account:

- **The charity must have powers to set up a subsidiary.** Usually these are there in the governing document, but it may be necessary to change it, if that is allowed.

- **Not be too speculative.** The Trustees should not be gambling with charitable money. There must be a robust business plan which will deliver **clear benefits to the charity**

- **Money can be lent to the subsidiary by the charity at a reasonable rate of interest** – at least as much as it would get from putting the money in a savings account. No subsidy from the parent Charity is allowed. Charitable money should be used for the charity's objects, not to set up a trading activity.

- Obviously, there has to be **separate accounting,** and there is a good case for separating the management and governance. Some of the Trustees of the main charity should sit on the subsidiary's Board, but not all of them and there should be independent Board members of the subsidiary who are not Trustees. This avoids those, hopefully rare, occasions when the interests of the charity and its subsidiary conflict.

Why bother being a charity?

Why should a Social Enterprise be a charity? One simple reason for many organisations is that they have to be. If an organisation is doing charitable activities it **has** to declare itself a charity and register with the Charity Commission if its turnover is greater than £5,000. Until 2007, the limit was £1,000. If the turnover is below the cut-off figure, then registration is not required, but the Charity Commission still has jurisdiction and can step in should there be problems.

However the usual reason is to be able to **access more funds**. A charity has many more places to go for money than the average not-for-profit organisation without charitable status.

There are over 2,500 **grant-giving trusts** in England and Wales alone, let alone Scotland and Northern Ireland. These are charities set up over the past few hundred years to distribute money to make the world a better place. Many of these trusts are constrained by their objects only to give money to charities. Others restrict themselves voluntarily to grants to charities, because it is administratively easier. Their rationale is that a charity is being regulated; someone is checking that they are operating properly; and they need to do less due diligence of their own.

These benefits should be used with care. As I mentioned, the essence of Social Enterprise is in being a business. Becoming a charity raises the temptation to rely on grants and gifts to survive which could stifle the entrepreneurial spirit.

Of course, the essence of Social Enterprise is that most funds will be generated from enterprise, but if someone may give you a grant to pay for what you want to do, then you are not going to turn it down are you?

The major use of a grant for a Social Enterprise is to try new activities. A three-year setting up grant for a new, potentially risky project is a very good way of testing the water without threatening the family silver. The danger lies in becoming dependent on the grant, which usually has a finite end.

Another reason for being a charity is the **tax breaks** available when individuals give money to a charity. If an income tax payer gives money to charity, the charity can claim back the tax paid on earning it, and the individual can claim back the higher rate tax paid on their tax return. Money left to a charity in a legacy is not subject to inheritance tax. There are also major savings on capital gains tax if shares or property are donated to a charity.

A donation from a company to a charity is made before corporation tax is paid, which reduces the cost of a donation considerably.

Finally, charities have automatic concession on **business rates** on premises. Charities can get 85% business rate relief on their premises, and most local authorities waive the other 15%. Not-for-profit organisations can often get this rate relief too if they can persuade their local authorities that they are sufficiently deserving, but it is not a right.

4. Why Social Enterprise Matters

At its best Social Enterprise is a brilliant way of combining all these ingredients to be a force for good:

- enterprise
- community
- social purpose
- business
- passion

It is a different way of doing business, creating wealth while increasing social capital.

At the beginning of this book, I talked about some of the things that identify Social Enterprises:

- working in places others do not want to

- employing people others do not wish to

- doing things that others do not want to

Profits are important, but it is what you do with them that counts.

Conventional private businesses have noticed that customers are increasingly looking for more from their suppliers than just the goods or services they need. The perceived social, environmental and ethical positions of companies are important when purchasing decisions are being made. Corporate Social Responsibility is a major selling point. Social Enterprises have this embedded in the way the organisation works, not added on as an afterthought.

a. Wealth Creation

A major reason Social Enterprise matters is because it allows for **wealth creation** with an overtly social aim.

The third sector, particularly the voluntary sector, is good at **spending** money. That is what it is largely set up to do. It provides care for older people; people with disabilities; it runs a hospice. It does this using funds obtained from the general public or grants from government, local or central. These are activities that consume money, not create it.

It spends money generated elsewhere - from individual people's income; from money raised as taxes; from private company profits or from interest accrued on endowments held by charitable trusts.

Social Enterprise, like all enterprise, is about creating wealth. It is about **making** money rather than spending it. This is very important for the economy of a country, a region or even a small community.

b. Money leaks from communities

There are many communities in the UK where no wealth is created. There are no local businesses to bring fresh money into the local economy. The money which circulates comes as benefits to the unemployed or those considered not fit for work. On many social housing estates, the only legal enterprises are the Post Office, a general store and a fast food outlet. Often all three are combined in one unit. The owner lives elsewhere. Money circulates to a limited extent and then leaves the community.

Enterprise is limited to the so-called "black" economy. Jobs are done cash-in-hand to avoid the eye of the state.

Community Enterprises have a real role to play here. It is often the only way to get out of dependency.

c. Empowering people

Social Enterprise, particularly small ones are often started by people who have a passion, but little idea of what they are taking on, and sometimes no real understanding of business. If they are to succeed, they have to pick that up of course, because they are operating "real" businesses in a real world. However, because they may not know how "real" businesses work, they are prepared to do things differently, and not only employ people others do not want, but also to help them to work beyond what is conventionally expected of them. Social Firms, employing people with disabilities, physical or developmental or mental health service users or ex-offenders, are very good at doing this. It is very easy to underestimate an individual's potential.

Many Social Enterprises have very democratic structures. This is inherent in cooperatives, for example, with each member having an equal say. They have many more stakeholders than a conventional business. A whole village may be able to make its voice heard.

d. Avoiding grant-dependency

One of the major problems for small community organisations and charities is survival. Often they get a start-up grant from a funder – a local authority, a charitable trust or one of the arms of the National Lottery. The difficulty is that the grant is usually time dependent and may not be renewed.

It is common for organisations to go through a three year cycle of feast and famine. They have a three year grant, develop services and then close them down and make all the staff redundant. Some organisations I have worked with refuse to put their beneficiaries through the process of providing a brilliant service, raising expectations and then dashing all hopes and closing down. They feel it is better to provide something which is less good, but always there, rather than yo-yoing between excellence and nothing.

Social Enterprise can provide an income stream which is steady and less dependent on the whim of funders.

However, sometimes expectations are too high. One small charity with a turnover of £150,000 – all short-term grants from a local authority - a year wanted me to recommend how to become a Social Enterprise which would deliver a profit to replace that funding. The manager had no entrepreneurial skills or experience, and no financial assets for start-up. I assured her that if such a business existed off the peg I would be setting it up for myself, rather than earning my living advising third sector organisations.

e. Positive effect on mainstream business

Social Enterprises make a virtue of the added social value they provide over and above the money that they make. Cooperative Bank with its ethical banking standards is a good example of this.

Mainstream businesses see this makes good business sense and modify their products and services accordingly.

The whole idea of Corporate Social Responsibility has become much more important in this context. If a social business is getting more sales, then its competitors will surely follow.

5. Here be Dragons – Watch out!

In 2007, a Social Enterprise support organisation asked those who attended its annual conference to describe what animal they saw their Social Enterprise as, and what animal they saw private business as. They were appalled at the answers. So much so that they decided it would not be sensible to publish them.

The Social Enterprises saw themselves as cuddly koalas or fluffy rabbits.

Their view of the private sector: ravening wolves; foxes out to deceive; tigers ready to eat you.

> *Third sector* – Social – Charity - friendly – nice

> *Private Sector* – nasty money-grubbing – dangerous

This is a very worrying mindset. The whole ethos of Social Enterprise is that it is enterprise; that it works in the real business world. Yet the people doing it are not comfortable with their idea of what business is about.

One business adviser said to me: "If a business model doesn't stack up, then we can call it a Social Enterprise and apply for some support grants." On the contrary, if a business plan does not stack up, it will work neither as a private business nor as a Social Enterprise.

Should it be a Social Enterprise at all? – The issue of control

Just because you want to do good does not mean you need to set up a Social Enterprise. You may be better off starting a charity or setting up a conventional private business.

One of the major issues is control. It is difficult for one person to remain in control of a Social Enterprise, or a charity for that matter. There may be a charismatic leader, but control lies ultimately with a Board. It is difficult to be a social entrepreneur on your own.

If you want to keep charge of everything and be your own boss, then you must set up a private business which you can do what you like with. This can be a socially aware business and do great good, but it will not be a Social Enterprise.

The alternative, which I do not advise, is to set up your Social Enterprise with a Board you can bully and cajole into doing exactly what you want. There are many organisations like this, but there are huge dangers here. The social aspect of Social Enterprise is very important and the checks and balances are there for a reason. One senior person in a charity once said to me, when I queried the legality of some of their business practices: "We do good for people with learning disabilities. We can do what we like."

Social Enterprises are the result of a group of people deciding to act together. Sometimes they are inspired by an individual, but it is a group activity.

Thinking small

The quiz at the beginning of this book highlighted some very large, well-established businesses which could be said to meet the definition of Social Enterprise.

Social Enterprises start small, just as all businesses do. However, too many of them stay small. Some of this is because it has been difficult in the past to access the finance to get bigger, but in many cases it is a lack of self-belief that such a thing is possible.

They are not alone. Most small private businesses do not aspire to be vast. There are still local corner shops and fast-food takeaways, which do not aspire to be Tesco or Burger King. The idea of a second shop or expansion where they are, is a step too far from their comfort-zone.

On the other hand, some Social Enterprises may also decide that one shop is quite enough – not everyone wants to rule the world. If that is a conscious decision, then so be it. The sad fact is that, because of the group control of Social Enterprise, and sometimes the use of public funds, many are actually much less willing to take risks than private companies.

Fear of professionalism

People often (usually?) become Social Entrepreneurs or set up Social Enterprises or charities by accident. Something captures them and drives them forward.

The birth of a child with a particular condition led Judy Fryd to write to Nursery World magazine in 1946, to suggest the idea that parents of children with learning disabilities could work together to form an organisation which would be listened to. This was the beginning of Mencap, the largest charity in the UK for people with learning disabilities.

By 2007, Mencap had 58 districts throughout the UK which are run by volunteer committees. It also employed 4,500 people in a series of business units. Mencap has contracts with various public bodies for delivering services, as well as raising funds from the general public. It is a business with a turnover of £178 million.

At least 600,000 people are employed in the third sector in the UK. This is more than are employed in agriculture in the UK.

There is a potential conflict here between those who give their time freely for the common good, and those who work in the sector and have families to feed and mortgages to pay.

A lot of the decision-making is done by those giving time voluntarily. Sometimes they expect this selflessness on the part of their employees. There are passionate paid workers in the third sector, who are prepared to take less money and work antisocial hours because of the cause they work for, but there are many more who are there because they need a job. Being a Social Enterprise still means meeting all the tedious red tape of running a business – employee liability insurance, health and safety law and so on. It may be run by volunteers, but that does not mean it must be amateur.

Being professional does not mean that all social awareness and passion is lost. The best Social Enterprises are passionate and run properly to high standards.

Politicians – acceptable privatisation?

A relatively recent source of Social Enterprise is a legacy of the major drive in the 1980's and a1990's to privatise public services. British Gas, British Telecom and other utilities became private companies as the State created public companies and sold the shares in them. The theory was that private businesses would be better run than public monopolies.

Most of these new private companies were successful and still exist. A few came to grief, and are now effectively large Social Enterprises constituted as companies limited by guarantee reinvesting their profits in their businesses. Network Rail which runs the UK rail infrastructure and Glas Cymru, the holding company of Welsh Water which provides water and sewage services in Wales are two major examples.

This form of privatisation was not acceptable to the Labour Government which took over in the mid 1990's. What is acceptable is transferring services to Social Enterprises.

The Housing Association movement was the first major wave as they took over the provision of social housing from councils. They were free to borrow to build when councils were constrained by strict public sector borrowing limits. The more recent trend has been stock transfer, where council housing has been transferred to Social Enterprises set up for the purpose. Many councils in the UK now have little or no housing stock. The rationale here is the same, a housing association can borrow to bring houses up to standard, in a way councils cannot.

Another major area is the provision of leisure centres. This started in 1993 when the London Borough of Greenwich transferred its leisure centres to Greenwich Leisure Limited, an Industrial and Provident Society. This company now runs sixty-five leisure centres throughout London. The idea spread and now the Sports and Recreation Trust Association (SpoRTA) which was founded in 1997 has a membership of over 115 leisure trusts from all parts of the UK. Together the trusts have a combined annual turnover in excess of £525 million, have over

205 million customers visiting their facilities each year and employ over 25,000 full time employees. They operate over 800 individual sites.

Two of these Trusts - Trafford Community Leisure Trust and Wigan Leisure and Culture Trust are also registered charities. The latter runs the cemeteries and a crematorium as well as leisure facilities.

By and large these leisure trusts are able to run leisure centres at lower costs and at higher standards than the councils which still own the premises which they lease to them. Public services are now being delivered by Social Enterprise rather than by councils.

These successes have spurred on the UK Government to apply the idea in other sectors of service delivery. A special unit has been set up to assist parts of the National Health Service in England to hive off as Social Enterprises. Local councils are being encouraged to contract out care services to charities or Social Enterprises.

One issue with this is the need for entrepreneurship and risk-taking in the management which takes over the new business. Middle managers with a social care background may not be the most obviously entrepreneurial people. The contracts these firms have initially will in due course be submitted to open tender. Are they going to be able to compete against the large private health and social care suppliers who will be going after a larger share of the market?

But above all, do they have the passion to change the world? My heart fails when I discover that an organisation which wants my advice is full of tepid and well-meaning individuals as employees and as volunteers.

6. Practicalities

a. First Find your Social Entrepreneur

As with any business, there has to be someone who cares enough to set it up and drive it forward. But Social Enterprises are special beasts. They need to be business savvy, but they also need to have empathy for the other intangibles I have been talking about.

I have a profoundly politically incorrect view that the most effective Social Enterprises and the best charities are created and led by people who are at least slightly unhinged. They are people who do not accept that it is impossible to employ people with learning disabilities at a normal wage doing normal jobs. They are people like Tim Smit who would not accept that it was not possible to turn some old clay-pits in Cornwall into the glass domes of the Eden project.

Is it possible to create a social entrepreneur? Are they born not made? The debate continues, just as it does in the world of "real" business. How many Richard Bransons can the world cope with?

Sometimes the founder stays with the organisation; sometimes they move on and found more than one. Michael Young could probably claim to be the most prolific of UK Social entrepreneurs with, among other things, the mad ideas of the Open University, the Consumers Association, the University of the Third Age, the National Consumer Council and the School for Social Entrepreneurs, among others.

On a smaller scale you have the artist William Wilkins who lives next door to the most romantic of medieval castles – Carreg Cennen, in rural Carmarthenshire - and created first the National Botanic Garden of Wales with its magnificent great glasshouse, is now busily restoring the gardens at Aberglasney a few miles away, and not content with this created one of the world's most lucrative fine arts prizes – Artes Mundi.

You can teach people the basics of business and the intricacies of charity law, but you cannot create the fire and inspiration. Sadly that explains why many Social Enterprises have fallen by the wayside. Not many social workers make good entrepreneurs. Indeed it could be the very characteristics which make them excellent social workers which make them poor business people.

Another factor to bear in mind is that different characteristics are needed to **create** a Social Enterprise from those required to **run** one. Those who create the business may not be the ones to keep it going after the excitement of starting up a new venture.

b. When should you set up a Social Enterprise?

Key ingredients:

- You need an idea for a **business** which has a strong **social component.**

- You want to share responsibility for turning the idea into reality.

- You have identified (cajoled) some people to come in with you.

- You have a good idea as to how you propose to do it.

The next requirement is a strong business plan which will convince you and all the people whose support you need to get it going.

You can then use the business plan with confidence to help raise the finance you need to get started. The places to look for money are outlined in Chapter 7.

The important point at each phase is to create a reality check. It is all too easy to get carried along by a brilliant idea without pausing to see if it can really work. Would it be better all round if you set up a conventional business and just gave the profits to an existing charity?

Do not get hung up about the structure and constitutional framework too early in the process. Work out what you want to do and then decide if being a charity or a cooperative will help or hinder.

Work out a clear action plan at the outset and try to stick to it.

c. How do you know it matters? - Social Audit

The financial figures will give you a good idea of how well a Social Enterprise is doing, but it is only half the story. That tells you all about the **enterprise** part. It does not tell you about the **social** part.

Social Audit is the buzz word for the process of deciding how well a Social Enterprise is tackling its social remit. This is a process by which an organisation:

- Accounts for its social performance

- Reports on and improves that performance

- Assesses its social impact and ethical behaviour in relation to its aims and those of its stakeholders.

At its broadest, it is used to capture the whole set of values, issues and processes that must be addressed in order to minimize any harm resulting from any activities and to create economic, social and environmental value.

At its narrowest, the term **triple bottom line** is used as a framework for measuring and reporting performance against three factors:

- Economic
- Social
- Environmental parameters.

Unlike the strictures laid down in the Companies Act and the various Statements of Recommended Practice to be followed in drawing up financial accounts for private businesses, there is no consensus on precisely what a social audit should be. I recently went to an event where we were presented with a computer disk with twelve different methods for social audits of varying complexity.

51

What they all boil down to is being clear about the social purpose, being able to measure it in some way, and taking into consideration the needs of all the organisation's stakeholders, which can be:

- Customers
- Employees
- Business partners
- Local communities
- The general public
- Governments, local. regional or national.

Under the Charities Act 2006, charities will have to make a statement of Public Benefit on an annual basis. Community Interest Companies will have to provide a Community Benefit statement.

What is important is not to lose sight of the wider goal the Social Enterprise had in the first place. How has it changed the world for the better in the past year?

There is a danger on focussing on **outputs** which are relatively easily measurable rather than **outcomes** which are more intangible and overall **impact**.

To make clear the distinction: If I run a series of workshops on fundraising for charities in Wales, my **outputs** are the number of people on each workshop and the number of workshops. My **outcomes** are individuals who can go back to their charities and are fired up to get greater funds for the causes they believe in. The **impact** is a Wales in which revitalised charities are making a real difference to people's lives.

The Cooperative Bank has a highly sophisticated report every year which enumerates the quantity of paper recycled, the environmental credentials of suppliers, the fundraising activities of its staff, the ethical stance on selecting customers and much more.

Social audit can be simple or sophisticated, but its purpose is to demonstrate that a Social Enterprise has made a real difference.

7. Funding for Social Enterprises

Where do you get the money to set up your Social Enterprise? The first place to look is to do what all enterprises do whether they are social or not – the founder, their family, friends and acquaintances, their bank, government schemes to support enterprise.

But everything is not always plain sailing. Even when you have a strong business plan, banks tend to be wary of a company which is not just there to make money.

One Social Enterprise with which I have been working for the past ten years needed to expand from very ropey premises to shiny new larger ones. We had a solid business plan and had been with one of the big four UK banks for ten years. We had never borrowed from them and had built up a small nest egg, but not enough to fund our expansion. Their view when approached for a loan was that they did not know what a company limited by guarantee was. They did not like the look of them and would not lend without personal guarantees from the directors.

We ended up borrowing from a funder which specialises in cooperatives – ICOF (Independent Common Ownership Fund) now known as Cooperative and Community Finance. Our business plan was rather wide of the mark. We had not expected the success. Within twelve months we had hit our three year targets, and needed three industrial units rather than the individual unit we had tentatively moved to. After eighteen months we had moved to a unit ten times bigger than the large one we had agonised over. We paid for this expansion and made all the repayments on the loan on time.

The most important item in getting funding is a business plan which holds water. Without this, no-one will lend and you had better give up now. You may need some start-up seed money, as all businesses do, and because of your social aims, you may be able to get a charitable grant if you cannot get the usual business support grants available to all new enterprises.

But you must have a plan which shows a sustainable long-term income stream which does not depend on dollops of external grant funding.

The big commercial banks are now much more amenable to the idea of Social Enterprise. They scent a profitable market. Head office should be able to help even if the local branch manager is less clued up.

These are the specialist lenders to Social Enterprises:

- **The Cooperative Bank,** as you would expect.

- **Unity Trust Bank** which is owned by the trade union movement.

- **Triodos Bank** which was set up in 1980 in the Netherlands and opened its UK operation in 1994.

- **Charity Bank** which is the only bank which is also a registered charity.

There are also various initiatives from government specific to Social Enterprises, some national and some regional. These are over and above the government grants and loans available to any business initiative.

If the Social Enterprise has charitable status then it may be possible to obtain grant funding from charitable trusts. For the right project, the Arts Councils and Sports Councils may be able to assist.

Then there is the possibility of applying to the various National Lottery bodies:

- Big Lottery Fund which funds social projects UK-wide

- The Heritage Lottery Fund

- The arts and sports lottery bodies in each country

- The UK Film Council

- NESTA – The National Endowment for Sports and the Arts.

For an individual starting out as a potential Social Entrepreneur, small grants are available from UnLtd - www.unltd.org.uk

There are also now a number of specialist providers of investment for social enterprises such as:

o   Big Issue Invest

o   Bridges Ventures

o   Venturesome

o   Community Development Finance Institutions (CDFIs)

o   Cooperative and Community Finance

o   Adventure Capital Fund

o   Social Investment Scotland

o   Finance Wales Community Loan Fund

8. The Future

Social Enterprise matters because it is a different way of thinking about business, charity, capitalism, employment. To use the business-speak, **it is a different model of business.** At its best it engages and enthuses people in a way that other business models often do not.

Look at the range of Social Enterprise champions:

- **Politicians** who see a way of introducing private enterprise ideas into the management of public services, but without the political downside of privatisation.

- **Grant-dependent voluntary organisations** who see a new sort of income without restrictive strings.

- **Ideologues on the left** who see a way of making business methods palatable and empowering communities and workers.

- **Ideologues on the right** who see business and enterprise as the cure for social ills.

- **Social Service departments** who see a way of moving people with disabilities into the labour market.

- **Community activists** who see ways of preserving the closing school in the village or keeping the village post office or general store open.

I also see more organisations which, like some of those whose examples I used in the quiz earlier on in this book, may not think of themselves as Social Enterprises. Take **the Guardian newspaper**, which is published by Guardian Media Group plc, owned by the Scott Trust, whose purpose is:

- To secure the financial and editorial independence of the Guardian in perpetuity: as a quality national newspaper without party affiliation; remaining faithful to its liberal tradition; as a profit-seeking enterprise managed in an efficient and cost-effective manner.

- All other activities should be consistent with the central objective. The Company which the Trust owns should: be managed to ensure profits are available to further the central objective; not invest in activities which conflict with the values and principles of the Trust.

- The values and principles of the Trust should be upheld throughout the Group. The Trust declares a subsidiary interest in promoting the causes of freedom in the press and liberal journalism, both in Britain and elsewhere.

I cannot resist quoting the injunction given to all new Guardian editors, which is to conduct the paper *'on the same lines and in the same spirit as heretofore.'*

GMG is a very successful – not to say aggressive company in a very competitive field whose profits are used to maintain a newspaper with a social conscience. Definitely a Social Enterprise in my book.

Encouragement from Government

There is likely to be even more pressure on the public sector both to create more Social Enterprises or to contract with Social Enterprises for delivery of services.

As they become more sophisticated, larger Social Enterprises will be created to or grow organically to compete with large private companies. This is already being seen in the rise of Greenwich Leisure in London and ECT (Ealing Community Transport) which are now major players in engineering and recycling as well as commercial bus services and community transport.

New ways of working

The development of the internet provides an opportunity for new Social Enterprises just as it has for private enterprises. Two exciting examples are:

- **Zopa** which is an online brokerage service, matching together lenders and borrowers.– www.zopa.com

  This is Social Lending, where people lend and borrow money with each other, without involving banks. Zopa conducts the required credit checks and allows individuals to lend money to each other at agreed rates of interest, taking a small percentage cut to pay for its overheads.

- **Freshties** is "where people swap, share, give and take." www.freshties.com

  It creates services to:

  - Let people help their community in ways that suit them.
  - Generate money for communities.

  "FreshTies unites people to make the most of their experiences, support, resources, and build real community. And it all starts in your area, as everyone has something to offer and gain."

There is huge scope for using the web for social purposes. These are only the start.

✱   ⁂   ✳   ✳   ✳   ✳   ✳

Social Enterprise is a different way of looking at how building wealth can be used for social aims. It is a different way of using the profit from enterprise. It is now becoming a major player in our business economy. Watch out, because it does matter a lot.

Appendix 1 Further Reading

Books

Social Enterprise in Anytown
John Pearce
ISBN 978-0903319973 Calouste Gulbenkian Foundation, UK 2003

The Social Entrepreneur: Making Communities Work
Andrew Mawson
ISBN 978-1843546610 Atlantic Books 2008

Your Chance to Change the World: The No-fibbing Guide to Social Entrepreneurship
Craig Dearden-Phillips
ISBN 978-1903991930 Directory of Social Change 2008

Enterprising Nonprofits: A Toolkit for Social Entrepreneurs
J Gregory Dees; Jed Emerson; Peter Economy
ISBN 978 0471397359 John Wiley and Sons Inc 2001

Strategic Tools for Social Entrepreneurs: Enhancing the Performance of Your Enterprising Nonprofit
J Gregory Dees; Jed Emerson; Peter Economy
ISBN 978-0471150688 John Wiley and Sons Inc 2002

Keeping it Legal: legal forms for Social Enterprise
Bates, Wells & Braithwaite
ISBN 0-954361105 Social Enterprise London

Magazines

Social Enterprise
www.socialenterprisemag.co.uk/

New Sector
www.newsector.co.uk

New Start Magazine

www.newstartmag.co.uk/

Third Sector

Published by Haymarket   www.thirdsector.co.uk

Cooperatives Magazine

Published by Cooperatives UK www.cooperatives-uk.coop

Appendix 2 Definitions of Social Enterprise

- ### Department of Trade and Industry

Social Enterprises are businesses with primarily social objectives whose surpluses are principally reinvested for that purpose in the business or in the community, rather than being driven by the need to maximise profit for shareholders and owners.

Social Enterprises tackle a wide range of social and environmental issues and operate in all parts of the economy. By using business solutions to achieve public good, the Government believes that Social Enterprises have a distinct and valuable role to play in helping create a strong, sustainable and socially inclusive economy.

Social Enterprises are diverse. They include local community enterprises, social firms, mutual organizations such as cooperatives and large scale organizations operating nationally or internationally. There is no single legal model for Social Enterprise. They include companies limited by guarantee, industrial and provident societies and companies limited by shares; some organisations are unincorporated and others are registered charities.

- ### Social Enterprise Coalition – www.socialenterprise.org.uk

Social Enterprises are businesses that trade in the market with a social purpose. They use business tools and techniques to achieve social aims and include an incredibly wide range of organisations, for example cooperatives, development trusts, community enterprises, housing associations, social firms, and leisure trusts.

Defining Social Enterprise in more detail...

The simplest definition of Social Enterprise - as business trading in the market for a social purpose - allows for a wide range of interpretations and there is still an ongoing debate among practitioners and academics over the exact definition of Social Enterprise.

The Social Enterprise Coalition's view is that a Social Enterprise is not defined by its legal status but by its nature: its social aims and outcomes, the basis on which its social mission is embedded in its structure and governance, and the way it uses the profits it generates through its trading activities. It is helpful to consider some of the common characteristics that Social Enterprises display:

- Enterprise Orientation - they are directly involved in producing goods or providing services to a market.

- Social Aims - they have explicit social aims such as job creation, training or the provision of local services. Their ethical values may include a commitment to building skills in local communities. Their profits are principally reinvested to achieve their social objectives.

- Many Social Enterprises are also characterised by their social ownership. They are autonomous organisations whose governance and ownership structures are normally based on participation by stakeholder groups (eg employees, users, clients, local community groups and social investors) or by trustees or directors who control the enterprise on behalf of a wider group of stakeholders. They are accountable to their stakeholders and the wider community for their social, environmental and economic impact. Profits can be distributed as profit sharing to stakeholders or used for the benefit of the community.

- **Scottish Borders Social Enterprise Group -**
  www.scotborders.gov.uk

There are six defining characteristics fundamental to Social Enterprise (Source: "Social Enterprise in Anytown" by John Pearce):

- having a social purpose or purposes

- achieving the social purposes by, at least in part, engaging in trade in the marketplace

- not distributing profits to individuals

- holding assets and wealth in trust for community benefit

- democratically involving members of its constituency in the governance of the organisation

- being independent organisations accountable to a defined constituency and to the wider community.

The following detail might also be said to be crucial:

- Social Enterprises seek to be viable trading concerns making an operating surplus (Source: Introducing Social Enterprise (Social Enterprise London 2001))

- they are entrepreneurial in attitude.

- **Community Action Network –** www.can-online.org.uk

Many people use the term 'not-for-profit'; CAN tries to avoid this phrase simply because if you are not for profit, you are for loss, and if you are for loss, you go bust! Profits or, if you prefer, surpluses are a good thing. Without a profit you can't invest in improving the service to customers or grow the business. The question is what you do with the profit, how the wealth that is created is shared.

People are increasingly talking about social auditing. Some think this is a rigorous process that will lead to clear measurements, other people think it is an exercise in 'spin', with a lack of definition similar to corporate social responsibility.

Some people now refer to the 'triple bottom line', financially, socially and environmentally successful. Some people however find that the 'triple bottom line' conjures up unfortunate visual images. It's up to you!

Many CAN members are making the difficult transition from organisations that receive most of their funds from grants, to genuine sustainable trading entities. CAN has therefore decided to focus on supporting Social Enterprise to grow and thrive, rather than questions of definitions and audit.

- **Community Enterprise Wales -** www.communityenterprisewales.com

Community Enterprise is a process, in which people work together in their communities to develop the capacity to undertake commercial activities that are often missing. In many cases the needs are identified by the communities.

The businesses they create are managed by a volunteer board of directors on behalf of the community; as with private businesses, staff handle the day to day running.

The Board are responsible for the training and volunteering opportunities for all staff, as well as capital acquisition for the business which is then in community ownership.

Community Enterprise provides opportunities for people, often in disadvantaged communities, who have no previous knowledge or interest in business, to become involved in economic activity. It also gives local people an avenue for practical input into the economic and social well being of their community.

It translates community development into local job creation in many cases.

Community Enterprise can turn a local community group into a Community Business -a Company Limited by Guarantee, a Credit Union, a Social Firm or a Cooperative.

Appendix 3 Cooperative Values and Principles

The cooperative principles are guidelines by which cooperatives put their **values into practice:**

1. Voluntary and Open Membership

Cooperatives are voluntary organisations, open to all persons able to use their services and willing to accept responsibilities of membership, without gender, social, racial, political, or religious discrimination.

2. Democratic Member Control

Cooperatives are democratic organisations controlled by their members, who actively participate in setting their policies and making decisions. Men and women serving as elected representatives are accountable to the membership. In primary cooperatives members have equal voting rights (one member, one vote), and cooperatives at other levels are also organised in a democratic manner.

3. Member Economic Participation

Members contribute equitably to, and democratically control, the capital of their cooperative. At least part of that capital is usually the common property of the cooperative. Members usually receive limited compensation, if any, on capital subscribed as a condition of membership. Members allocate surpluses for any of the following purposes: developing their cooperative, possibly by setting up reserves, part of which at least would be indivisible; benefiting members in proportion to their transactions with the cooperative; and supporting other activities approved by the membership.

4. Autonomy and Independence

Cooperatives are autonomous, self-help organisations controlled by their members. If they enter into agreements with other organisations, including governments, or raise capital from external sources, they do so on terms that ensure democratic control by their members and maintain their cooperative autonomy.

5. Education, Training and Information

Cooperatives provide education and training for their members, elected representatives, managers and employees so they can contribute effectively to the development of their cooperatives. They inform the general public - particularly young people and opinion leaders - about the nature and benefits of cooperation.

6. Cooperation Among Cooperatives

Cooperatives serve their members most effectively and strengthen the Cooperative Movement by working together through local, national, regional and international structures.

7. Concern for Community

Cooperatives work for the sustainable development of their communities through policies approved by their members.

This statement is periodically reviewed, and was last agreed in 1995, by the International Cooperative Alliance (ICA). The ICA is the global organisation bringing together the worldwide cooperative movement.

Appendix 4 Governance Structures for Social Enterprise

It is important to separate the different **philosophical** foundation of a Social Enterprise – whether it is a social firm or a cooperative, say - from its **legal** governance structure.

Most organisations start as unincorporated bodies and move to incorporation as they become established, enter into contracts or seek to limit liability. The incorporated legal structures available are:

- **Company Limited by Guarantee**
- **Company Limited by Shares**
- **Community Interest Company**
- **Industrial and Provident Society**
- **Charitable Incorporated Organisation**

Taking these in turn:

Company Limited by Guarantee (CLG)

- Members make a nominal contribution
- Memorandum and Articles lock in assets
- Can apply for charitable status

- Model constitutions are available for

  o Charities
  o Development Trusts
  o Cooperatives
  o Social Firms

Company limited by Shares (CLS)

- "Normal" companies
- Some charity trading subsidiaries – where the charity owns the shares

- Some Social Enterprises such as The Big Issue where the founder holds the shares and the Memorandum and Articles prevent distribution of profit.

Community Interest Company (CIC)

- Designed as a company for those wishing to establish Social Enterprises.

- Particularly suitable for those who wish to work within the relative freedom of the familiar limited company framework without either the private profit motive or charity status.

- An organisation wishing to be a CIC can choose one of three company forms:
  - private company limited by shares
  - limited by guarantee
  - public limited company

To ensure that they use their assets and profits for the community interest CICs will have some special, additional features:

- Restricted from distributing profits and assets to their members.

- Produce an annual community interest report, delivered with their accounts to Companies House and placed on the public record.

- Applications for registration will be made to the Registrar of Companies in the usual way, but before the company can be incorporated, the application will be referred to the Regulator who will consider whether the company is eligible for CIC status.

Industrial and Provident Society (IPS)

An industrial and provident society is an organisation conducting an industry, business or trade, either as a cooperative or for the benefit of the community, and which is registered under the Industrial and Provident Societies Act 1965.

Most Housing Associations arc IPSs, as are organisations which work in that field such as Care and Repair which enables older people to stay in their own homes by providing adaptations.

Charitable Incorporated Organisation (CIO)

This is a new legal entity being created under the 2006 Charities Act:

This will be an incorporated body which will report only to the Charity Commission and not to Companies House. This means that only one set of accounts will be required rather than the two sets required at present for companies limited by guarantee which are also charities.

The first CIO's are expected in mid 2010.

Appendix 5 - The pros and cons of the various legal governance structures

This is the position for England and Wales. Similar, but not identical forms apply in Scotland and Northern Ireland.

This section was prepared in conjunction with Margaret Underwood, whose assistance is gratefully acknowledged.

Charitable Status

This is possible for unincorporated organisations, which may be associations or trusts. It is also available for incorporated entities which can be companies limited by guarantee (CLG) or from mid 2010 charitable incorporated organisations (CIO's). Incorporation provides limited liability for Trustees.

If an organisation is carrying out charitable activities, then it must register by law with the Charity Commission if its turnover is greater than £5,000 per annum.

Advantages	Disadvantages
Can register with Her Majesty's Revenue and Customs for Gift Aid on donations from individuals	If a CLG then accountable to two regulatory bodies – Charities Commission and Companies House (CIOs will only be regulated by Charity Commission)
Some grant making organisations such as charitable trusts will only give money to charities	If a CLG need to produce accounts in two formats
Credibility with general public	Lack of credibility with commercial world who do not see charities as significant players compared with private sector
85% mandatory rate relief. (many local authorities will waive the other 15%	Need to prove public benefit and demonstrate this regularly to maintain status

Community Interest Companies

Advantages	Disadvantages
Only one regulator – the Regulator of CIC's, based at Companies House	Must satisfy a community interest test in order to be registered.
A company structure with limited liability	Annual report must include how the CIC has acted to pursue its community interest
Possible to be a CIC limited by shares and pay a dividend to investors up to a prescribed limit	Not possible to be a CIC and a charity or to change from CIC to charity
Assets will be preserved for the community	No special tax status Not eligible for gift aid
Can have paid directors	Not eligible for rate relief unless a local authority waives this because of community benefit

Unincorporated and charitable

Regulated by Charity Commission, has trustees who are individually liable for the activities of the organisation. It is possible to purchase Trustee Indemnity Insurance which can provide some protection to Trustees.

Advantages	Disadvantages	Potential for problems
Regulated by an external body – Charity Commission	If they want to make changes to their constitution they must get Charity Commission permission. Must make annual returns to the CC unless they fall below the threshold.	Lack of awareness of charity issues
Can receive charitable gifts and apply to select sources	Perceived as having access to a much wider range of funding than is actually available.	Can get into trouble for taking money from inappropriate sources
Status afforded by charity	Can only act within their charitable objects	Undertaking activities outside their charitable objects
The number of trustees can be small – 3	Limits experience or knowledge	Lack of sufficient experience or knowledge
Trustees appointed rather than elected leading to a self-perpetuating governing body	Limits outside influences – undemocratic	Exclusive and non-inclusive
Trustees can hold land or buildings	The trustees are individually liable and they individually hold the assets	Problems with land or buildings, maintenance,
Trustees can hold investments	The trustees are individually liable for any issues.	upkeep, proper use etc. Many Trustees are unaware of their roles and responsibilities.

Unincorporated organisation – but not a charity

Advantages	Disadvantages	Potential for problems
Uncomplicated / Flexible		Making changes just to chase funding
Can have a simple governing document without the need to consult lawyers or other advisors	Cannot enter into legal agreements or take legal action in the name of the organisation – has to be done by individuals.	Difficulties in accepting gifts – clarity of use or intent
Can be set up and wound up easily and cheaply	Here today – gone tomorrow; could be wound up when things get tough	No longer term commitment – what happens to the assets if any problems arise
Can create own rules without having to be bound by outside requirements	Not regulated by any external agency such as the Charity Commission	They may be more unfamiliar with good practice issues
Rules can be changed quickly and easily of the original governing document includes procedures for amendment		
Privacy and absence of external accountability	Unlimited personal liability Individuals liable for debts of the group. Could lose their privacy by entering into agreements with third parties e.g. funders therefore becoming externally accountable	No external monitoring of finances Management of funds may not meet funders needs
If it wants to be a membership organisation	Exclusive	Equal opportunities requirements

If the group does not expect to own property, land or employ staff, will have a secure income, not undertake risky or financially burdensome activities	Not able to own buildings or land except via holding trustees Unwise to employ staff	Employing staff Entering contracts Trustees die / resign, critical information is lost, expensive to replace
	If a gift is given to the organisation - they need to seek legal advice to check the terms of the gift – is it for charitable purposes which mean a *Trust* is created or is it for the sole benefit of the members?	

Incorporated organisations

An incorporated organisation - a company limited by guarantee or a charitable incorporated organisation - exists as a legal entity separate from its members. This gives it the right to own property, land, enter into legal agreements and take legal action in the name of the organisation instead of individuals.

Advantages	Disadvantages	Potential for problems
Company governed by directors in most situations have limited liability.	The protection of limited liability is extensive but it is not absolute. In some situations trustees may still be personally liable Extra responsibilities and liabilities involved. Company law requires set paperwork; any directors may be fined if the organisation does not comply with requirements There is also a cost attached to setting up a company and meeting the financial audit requirements.	Unaware of requirements of company law, thinking they have complete protection and no liability in law. If you do not comply with company law – Companies House can remove you from the register and all monies in the company bank account will be frozen AND THERE ARE FINES.
Creates in law a body corporate so there is no need for holding trustees to own land or enter legal agreements.	Accountable in law to the Registrar of Companies – details of finances and names of company directors are public	
Has permanent succession – no need to transfer deeds, contracts leases or other legal agreements to new signatories when trustees / directors change.	It must go through a formal process to bring it to an end, it cannot just fade away.	Risks of fines if not properly maintained.
Gives a flexible structure suitable for any size of organisation.	People within the organisation must be prepared to deal with the legal requirements.	

Industrial and Provident Societies

This structure is only available to bona fide cooperative societies or to voluntary organisations carrying on an industry trade or business for the benefit of the community. Many Housing Associations are IPSs.

Industrial and Provident Societies register with Mutual Societies Registration part of the Financial Services Authority under the Industrial and Provident societies Act 1965.

Advantages	Disadvantages	Potential for problems
Democratically run by its members – one member one vote	Not generally for *public benefit*. Benefits are usually limited to its members so any profits are shared within a closed membership	Lack of understanding about the uses of this kind of structure
	Registration process is slower and more costly than for companies	
Limited liability		
Right to own property and to take legal action in its own name		
Legislative requirements less than for a company.		
Use of model rules make registration less onerous		

If an I&P Society has charitable purposes, then it can register with Her Majesty's Revenue and Customs for Gift Aid tax reclamation as an exempt charity.

Sometimes funders find the concept of a charitable I&P Society difficult to understand.

Cooperatives

A genuine cooperative carries on a business or trade for the mutual benefit of its members

Model governing documents are available for:

Unincorporated Cooperative

Advantages	Disadvantages	Potential for problems
Democratically run by its members – one member one vote	Not generally for *public benefit*. Benefits are usually limited to its members so any profits are shared within a closed membership	Lack of understanding about the uses of this kind of structure

Incorporated Cooperatives

These are Companies Limited by Guarantee or Industrial and Provident Societies. The advantage of incorporation is limited liability protection.

81

Dr Martin Price, has been Director of Martin Price Associates since 1996. He is an experienced consultant, who has had a number of senior management roles in the Third Sector in Wales.

Dr Price is Chair of The Institute of Fundraising Cymru and a UK Trustee of the Institute. He is Vice-Chair of the BBC Wales Charity Advisory Forum, which advises on BBC Children in Need applications and allocates charity broadcasts in Wales.

He is a Board Member of the Development Trusts Association Wales and of Social Firms Wales.

He is non-executive Chair of the largest Social Firm in Wales – Pack-IT Ltd in Cardiff Bay, which employs people with learning disabilities. Pack-It was the European Social Firm of the Year 2009. For three years, he was a Trustee of a Cardiff-based charity – ABCD, which helps children and young people from ethnic minorities who have disabilities.

He ran the South Wales operation of The Prince's Youth Business Trust, helping some 400 disadvantaged young people into self-employment over a period of three years. He worked with Business in the Community in Wales, setting up Employee Volunteering schemes, forging links between companies and the voluntary sector. He set up the Fundraising Operation for Mencap in Wales in their Fiftieth Anniversary year.

He was Project Manager for HRH The Prince of Wales' Twenty-fifth Anniversary of his Investiture, organising Royal Visits and three garden parties at Castles around Wales. Dr Price has sixteen years experience at a senior level in the commercial sector with British Gas plc, acting as an internal consultant on Operational Research projects, Corporate Planning, Business Strategies, Management Buy-Outs and managed the Information Technology Centre for British Gas in Wales.

www.martinprice.com

For other
FFLAN
Books
on the Third Sector

Visit our Web site

www.fflan.com